SOUL DISCLOSURE

SOUL DISCLOSURE

100% Access

Dee Weldon Bird

Strategic Book Publishing and Rights Co.

Strategic Book Publishing & Rights Co., LLC
USA | Singapore
www.sbpra.net

For information about special discounts for bulk purchases, please contact Strategic Book Publishing and Rights Co. Special Sales, at bookorder@sbpra.net.

ISBN: 978-1-950015-57-3

AUTHOR'S NOTE

Words are never enough to infinitely explain the magic of the universe, as it is something you explore and experience through your soul. Words are merely an introduction. My words welcome you home, a home you never left.

www.deeweldonbird.com

ACKNOWLEDGEMENTS

I would like to thank my first guide, Ramini, for guiding me through the physical part of my journey.

You welcome birth as you enter Earth; I welcomed and faced what you call death.

The word *death*, which you view as dark with loss and mourning, I see as light. Death for me opened the biggest door I ever walked through—I was four years old. It was a journey of self-discovery, which I shared with you in my first book, *From Both Sides of the Fence: The Gifts in U*. As I continued to travel through the layers of my physical history, I reached another doorway through my soul: the universe.

This journey gave me the history not only of us but how Earth began, which I shared with you in my second book, *Connecting to Life's Compass: You're Not Lost, You Just Think You Are*.

On one of our last travels together, Ramini showed me the lectern room where he introduced me to my new guide, Acho. It was after this introduction that I began to piece together everything that I had been shown for the past fifty years, which brought me to my third book, *The Map of the Universe: A Traveler's Guide*. I would like to thank Acho as he continues sharing the magic of the universe so I can share it with you.

I also would like to thank my family: my husband, Kevin, and my children, Gemma, Charlotte, Leanne, and Courtney, for their continued love, support, and understanding as I worked on piecing it together.

I would like to also thank every soul that has connected with me physically, remotely, or soul to soul.

This leads me to the present day. This booklet, *Soul Disclosure*, has a piece of your soul in it.

TABLE OF CONTENTS

INTRODUCTION

As I travel from Earth to space, to our home in a universe not defined by a street address, and as I exit Earth, I am aware that the only luggage I need is in my soul, and I feel relaxed knowing I do not need to check in with any ticket or boarding pass. No queues to stand in or arguments sounding in my ears.

I am free in the comfort of my own soul to travel anywhere in the universe, without any limitation or borders. If you wish for these boundaries, you will have to create them for yourself.

As the familiar frequencies pass me at super-fast speed, I lay back in the comfort of my soul. Here's an idea of what it is like: When you stand in a transparent lift as it goes up, it looks like the outer walls are moving downward. Obviously the lift is very slow moving compared to how fast you move in the universe, and you don't need a lift in the universe, because you are *still* in your own soul while these frequencies pass you.

As my bilocation structure surrounds me, the only thing I wear is my smile. I expand my soul in space after the limitations of Earth. I did not survive Earth; I experienced it in all its glory.

Now at home, I have so much to tell other souls about structure Earth. Earth is not the only structure I have visited, but this structure stands out because of the transitional shift that is happening from the physical frequency to the connection of the soul frequency.

As I reach my destination, I see souls that are eager to see me on my return. Souls gather round me welcoming me with unconditional love. It feels like I never left. Excitedly they ask me, "Tell us about your trip to structure Earth."

CHAPTER ONE

STRUCTURE EARTH

As I connected with Earth, I first noticed how souls communicate. As you know, we use the language of the universe: the four elements of frequency. The universal language is still used but in a distorted way in which the souls on Earth are not even aware they are using it. The distortion took me a while to understand and remember.

The physical flesh—known as the body—is consuming to say the least. The body is a main focus of attention and there is no getting away from it. The soul knows when the physical body is tired, which is why it has to sleep.

I spent my first 14 years on Earth observing how souls interacted with one another. This is how distortion had a ripple effect. It didn't take long for me to realize that what people said did not match their actions. They hid from others what they really felt inside.

Life around me not only became distorted with disinformation, it caused guesswork among souls. I stayed true to my soul and did not enter the ripple effect of distortion. I stayed in my own space that I called my own little world in my soul. This protected me from being sucked into how other souls had chosen to live their lives, which limited them from accessing the whole of themselves.

At first I viewed the situations I found myself in as feeling like the black sheep of the family. What this saying means simply is that you don't fit in. I felt like an outcast and had to rely on my strength in my soul to keep going. I did not enjoy the first forty years of my life; it was a challenge facing my own experiences, not to mention the demands and expectations of other souls that crossed my path. I came across other views and opinions. I came across fear. Fear is in everything, in every word, in every action.

Trying to communicate soul to soul on Earth is very exhausting when the physical is in the way. Souls come with many layers of experiences, so it was like talking to a soul wrapped in cling film. I could see the other souls, but the other souls could not, because they had forgotten who they were and believed they were their physical body.

I could see straight through their physical flesh and saw their soul truth, which caused me many problems when speaking the truth while growing up. Souls on Earth say they want to know the truth, yet do not want to see or hear it. They take things personally and literally.

Whatever situation I found myself in, I chose to speak the truth, which took strength. I knew that I had nothing to hide, and I lived my life like an open book: what you see is what you get. Being honest with other souls was often considered threatening. If I gave unconditionally, I was asked if I had an ulterior motive or asked what I wanted in return. This really took me by surprise. I did not have a clue what they were going on about. I just could not remember what these things were. It shook me like a punch to the body that knocks you to the floor. It was like being on the frontline during war when I communicated with souls.

Souls are on guard and don't know who they can trust, choosing to go by a surface reflection. I learned how to swim against the wave of distortion and found my own way to mix with souls on Earth.

Visiting Earth during the transitional shift was like a rollercoaster ride. Souls forgot that the ride they are on—the one we call the journey of experience—is not the whole picture. Like any ride at the fairground, you know you cannot get off until someone stops the ride, which makes you feel out of control and out of your comfort zone. You are used to being in control, so having an experience on the rollercoaster of Earth makes you believe that you are out of control. You believe you have no choice. Like being on a rollercoaster, you think you have to sit still and put up and shut up, unless screaming in fear.

I was aware at a young age that those termed "adults" were like children themselves. These adults taught young souls about danger and fear mainly, and not about freedom of self-expression. Trust was an issue, not just with other souls they connected with, but towards themselves also. Fear also had affected every layer of life on Earth and spanned centuries.

When souls entered Earth, they forgot about the gifts inside of their soul. They unpacked everything to survive fear. Souls had forgotten that they came in peace with love in their hearts. Living with fear, they came prepared to fight the fear in their memory. It did not matter how many times they visited Earth, they viewed each visit as the first, unless they had a touch of déjà vu, and then they became curious to remember more.

Preoccupied with fighting, the souls on Earth forgot they were here for a unique, meaningful experience. Forgetting and not understanding that space surrounds frequency, they were seeing souls around them as if themselves. They focused on what they could see rather than what they felt. They paid attention only when they looked in a mirror when getting ready to go out or if the body needed medical care.

Distraction with distortion caused souls to feel separate from the universe. They viewed Earth as the only important structure with life on it. They even saw creatures and animals with a body different from theirs as separate.

Anything souls did not understand they feared. Fear, being everywhere, was like air to their lungs. Survival of the fittest became survival of fear. Forgetting the connection with soul, this fear became a feeling of empty space, like something was missing inside rather than a safe space we call home. Souls lived with fear and saw themselves as the image they gave to fear. Fear, worn like a mask, took on many labels as a disguise. To see the soul, you had to get through layers of fear with feelings from experiences that had been buried like what they call death.

The space in their external home was filled with material things that they viewed would keep them safe. Open space became enclosed space, with walls built and fences and gates erected to keep out what they feared. Living like this in limited space made them feel confined and hemmed in. They searched outside of themselves to find what they were looking for and bought more and more to fill the empty void they felt inside. They bought acres of land to build bigger houses in which to live, to give the feeling of expanded space they had forgotten in their souls.

They prayed for freedom and saw money as a way to buy their way out of limitation. Money created more of what they feared, because they did not trust themselves enough to trust what money gave to them. Protecting what they owned felt heavy, as if they were attached to a ball and chain that followed them with every step they took. Money became gold, a currency once held, disappearing in memory.

Technology took over the physical mind and corruption occurred like a virus from the gadgets they held in their hands.

Souls that once held the hands of children now hold technology. Separation anxiety rippled through their hands, not in fear of losing the hand that they held, but in fear of losing the life that they uploaded.

Souls had no space to call their own. They searched for space within the mainframe of media transferred to the living space they once called home. A private life became a media showcase. Magazines that changed homes transformed lives into a reality glossed over with filters. The faces of souls soon disappeared with the touch of a button and were recognized as a digital image rather than the genuine article.

Souls felt that a lifestyle of fear was closing in on them. They turned to alcohol and drugs and food to numb them from their suffocation. The air was toxic with fear, and they could no longer breathe the fresh air of the soul. The open space they once loved now became a closed space that made them feel shut out from life.

With nowhere left to run or hide from fear, souls started to drop like flies, exiting Earth with no reason, other than fear itself. Souls thought that if they exited Earth, they would be free from fear, forgetting that the four elements of frequency forget nothing in the universe and delete nothing, unlike gadgets.

Entering Earth again, the memory of fear came flooding back that a life lived in fear is to be faced in order to let go. Face your fears, and then you will understand the soul fears nothing. Your soul space is how you are infinitely defined in the universe. You are safe in your soul. You have all the space you need to express yourself freely without fear getting in your way. It always comes back to the self.

CHAPTER TWO

WHAT SOULS LOOK LIKE

On Earth, souls view the physical image of the body as its soul identity. When a soul is ready to exit Earth, it mourns the physical body it chose to connect with. It fears what is called death as the end, because it sees how the physical body is buried and discarded like rubbish. Unable to see the soul through the body, it fears the loss, not of the body, but of the soul, and that it will not be able to recognize the exited soul without being connected to the body that it vacated. Fear consumes death for this reason alone: fear they will not be reunited with loved ones. With the physical body now gone, how will they find a loved one they cannot see? The physical body is worn like a mask; the noise of fighting that fills the atmosphere from within, the time of day turning like clockwork without a second to spare, catching up with the day before, and holding on to the past while fearing the future.

Silence is deafening and has nothing to do with being bored but with a fear of missing out. Keeping busy by being distracted, provided souls with a distorted view of themselves. They lived a lifestyle of being on the run from their physical self, fearing they had nothing to run to. A Life of fear ground to a halt.

The energy transfer opened up and expanded a life souls loved. This caused the shell of fear to crack open, which exposed what souls had been searching for: the truth, so they could remember who they are. The physical veil fell from the body. The searching and fighting was over. The bigger picture revealed itself like the sun shining after a storm. Souls were ready to face their physical selves so they could let go of the physical distortion. The rollercoaster ride souls had been on for centuries was over. At first souls felt unsteady on their feet after stepping off the ride. It took a while for souls to get used to a life of freedom, created on solid foundations, rather than the life they had known full of twists and turns and uncertainty. No more repeats, just a different day.

The energy transfer opened up a life of space to be filled with the creative gifts carried in the soul. The transfer of energy was completed when the portal opened up in March and April 2018. The transition was about getting used to a new paradigm, one that they were creating, not one found in history books of old.

At first the memory of the physical played in the background like an echo. As the connection strengthened with the soul, the physical way of life was discarded like the physical body. Life opened doors for souls they were no longer afraid to walk through. As they entered the first door they opened—the portal of the soul—they felt the benefits straight away. They felt like a weight had been lifted from them. They felt spaced out. They felt happy to have access to the gifts in their soul knowing they had total control to access more when they were ready. They felt safe and knew money could not buy them what the soul offered them. They found things about the soul they thought were not humanly possible. They loved how connecting with the soul felt the more they connected with it.

Life became more crystal clear and tuned in, rather than out of sync with distortion. There was no going back to the way life had been on Earth. Even if the souls wanted to, the energy transfer made sure the rollercoaster ride would not surface again.

How a soul looks and feels is unique because of the frequency signature. There are no twin souls in the universe, because of the magic of space. Souls can be whatever they want to be.

When a soul chose to let go of the physical frequency to transfer and connect with the soul frequency during a soul reading, it took a nanosecond. How long the soul stayed in the soul pool after stripping from the physical for the first time, gave the soul a chance to get adjusted to being a soul without the physical getting in the way. Connecting with the soul is what exiting Earth feels like. Connecting during a soul reading does not mean an exit. When you have breath on Earth, you are still connected with the physical body. A doorway opened to the bigger picture of the universe, and each soul chose to walk through the portal of its unique soul to see the universe for itself. Soul readings were seen in a whole new light.

As each soul connected and remembered who it was, a domino effect was created that knocked out the frequency of fear. Souls that were connected saw the bigger picture of Earth. They saw the connection the physical did not see. They felt unconditional love toward themselves. They shared love with the reflection of souls around them. They created a life together in teamwork and not in competition. They enjoyed facing their experiences and completing them.

Life expanded on planet Earth with fresh new experiences and without the need for repeats. The old paradigm of fear started to crumble and fall to the ground. Anything that had previously been built on the platform of fear fell away. At first souls were confused, as they could feel that change was coming long before the portal opened up. The souls that were more connected shed the physical quickly, so they could support and guide other souls during the transition.

The landscape of Earth changed too. At first souls thought it was history repeating itself. Souls wanted to be free from the crumbling fear of distortion. They thought if they sped like they had in the past, they would be free, forgetting that what they create stays in their own space—you cannot run from your own creation. What they were running away from followed them until they stopped running and faced it.

Souls were taught in the old paradigm that food gave the physical body energy. They forgot that they are energy. They were told to eat at certain times of the day. This routine was set like an alarm clock that went off in the brain. Souls relied on the brain. They wrote their daily routine on a calendar so they could follow it. They created a timetable of schedules all planned and mapped out with little time left for themselves. The timetable of when to eat wasn't enough for the big businesses that sold food. They created dates that matched the timetable that souls recognized. Business in the food industry boomed.

They created labels that mapped out the number of calories a soul should follow as a gauge. This allowed souls to eat whatever they wanted within the guidelines set. As each century passed, the way souls ate changed, not by the seasons but by trends set within the food industry. Souls forgot the body required food to create more flesh for the body. If the body needed more muscle or skin, the cells within the body used what the soul ate for repair. It had nothing to do with energy.

The food industry had brainwashed souls into believing that the food they ate gave them the energy that the body needed. Truth stared them in the face; they would say they were in a food coma and needed a nap after consuming a big meal. They did not put two and two together.

If food gave souls energy, then souls would be running marathons continuously. The soul gets all the energy it needs through breathing and sleeping. A soul connects with the physical body at the first breath when the body is born. The baby body sleeps and eats a lot. Sleeping and breathing is energy for the soul; eating is so the baby can regenerate new cells and grow more.

Souls who experienced having children, often had a battle on their hands at meal times as they tried to get the children to eat. They taught the children how to eat within the guidelines set out in the food industry. It was not an easy challenge, so battles began between the children and the parents.

The baby souls knew they did not get energy from the food given to them. They knew they got all the energy they needed during sleep, which is why they woke up at the crack of dawn. They often don't want to eat because they are getting more sleep than the adults, and they are full on energy. Deep down the adult souls know this, because they encourage the children to sleep as part of their daily routine, saying, "You grow while you sleep."

Truth has always been in plain sight mixed with fear. Souls experienced how energy transfer works when they had a lot of work to do and didn't eat. These souls would say they were running on thin air or adrenalin. They noticed they had more energy than when they ate. It is like the soul kicks in with adrenalin, so they do not feel they need to eat to get a workload done. They know deep down inside that if they ate it would slow them down. The reason why they became drained was not because they had not eaten, but because they had burned the candle at both ends, resulting in a lack of sleep.

The soul does not sleep. It transfers energy to the body every second of every day with each breath that is taken. When you listen to your soul, they know what the body needs, not by the mind's program, but by the feeling received from inside. They might say, "I feel like having a banana today." The body was communicating to them what the body needed for repair.

When the physical body says "I think" or "I need," it knows it is the brain talking. If it had remembered that its brain does not have an off switch, it would have understood why it was hard to stop eating when listening to its brain. Mastering the physical brain is to master the connection with the soul.

The choice of what diet to follow became overwhelming for souls. They tried every diet going, not understanding why they didn't work long term. Souls had forgotten that they have a natural energy rhythm that does not need a timetable. This rhythm sounds not as an alarm but as a rumbling tummy. Souls were able to hear the sound as well as feel it. It had nothing to do with thinking. When the thinking/timetable lifestyle was created it was so loud that it distracted souls from the natural rhythm inside themselves. Souls invented watches to keep an eye on the time so they would not forget when to eat. A lifestyle was created that was unnatural to the soul. Souls ate so much they flooded the physical body with excess fat the body did not need to keep warm. The fat spread through every organ in the body, which caused stress and distress resulting in disease.

How souls ate matched what they believed about the food they had consumed. If they believed it was bad food or good food resulted in a mirror physical reaction. It was not because of the food itself, it was because of the energy label they gave to it.

Souls had forgotten the connection to everything, which gave them their experiences. The physical body is mostly water, like Earth is mostly water—a perfect match! You don't see Earth eating everything in sight. The landscape breathes and sleeps in the natural rhythm of life.

Souls even were taught to drink far more than the body needed. Too much of anything flushes something else out of the body that it needs. Vitamins were invented to try and balance out the body. The soul has everything it needs to have an enjoyable experience.

The new paradigm turned the tables on the systems that had consumed the souls for centuries. Souls listened to themselves rather than the systems that had controlled them. Life changed on Earth; natural instincts that hold all the wisdom of the universe surfaced from the manuscript in the soul. Souls put two and two together and created a lifestyle that matched the rhythm of the soul. The new paradigm created the landscape that matched the frequency signature of Earth. The souls saw Earth in its natural beauty. Souls did not take what they did not need. Souls lived in harmony with the landscape and that of nature and the animal kingdom, communicating together, and using the four elements of frequency. Souls remembered that everything they experience is soul, a reflection that is a rainbow spectrum of infinite creativity.

CHAPTER THREE

SOUL MAGNETISM – 100 PERCENT ACCESS

In the old paradigm the physical brain had access of 10 percent. This information was brainwashed into souls through the systems that had been created. The systems were not just a timetable to follow schedules in the days of the week but came with rules and regulations as well. Souls believed that they were the physical body and nothing more than that. They were taught that the 10 percent they accessed of the brain was 10 percent of the brain's function. They had forgotten that the brain is a pathway for neurons to transmit information to the body. This information network exchange is so the brain can receive what the body needed for repair; it had nothing to do with intelligence.

Souls believed, as they had been taught, that what they shared with the reflection of other souls came from the brain and not the soul. Souls that arrived on earth, who shared the gifts from the soul, did not match the members of the family. This left souls with more questions than answers. Souls that arrived naturally able to play the piano at three years old would have made Mozart the composer proud. Playing the composed pieces blew the adults' mind away. Even these geniuses were not enough to help souls remember who they were. They saw these souls as prize possessions in which to create easy money.

Over the centuries, souls have shared gifts from the soul in plain sight. Not understanding these gifted souls, they would either react as though gold had landed on their laps or burn them at the stake out of fear. A soul that stood out as being different would be valued and sought after with a high price on its head.

Souls that were rejected, not included, or abandoned in the community had no way of being welcomed back into the community. Word spread, making sure these feared souls would never return. A label created by a soul is a label carried by many.

What happens with the physical stays with the physical. You cannot mix the frequency of the physical with the frequency of the soul; it is a choice between the two. A body that is termed brain dead reflects the limitations of the physical body. The physical body does not function if the neurons cannot transmit information. The intelligence that the soul thought came from the brain is now replaced with frustration. Souls have defied the physical body by the sheer determination of the soul.

Souls viewed what they called a miracle and still did not remember who they were. Souls still believed they were the physical body regardless of the magic shared. The 10 percent accessed is actually the 10 percent of the soul that the soul has chosen to connect with.

With so much misinformation, souls became confused about what came from where. Souls that arrived on Earth forgot that they had 100 percent access to their soul. The network of the brain overshadowed the pathway of the soul causing it to be out of sync with the body.

Souls conditioned themselves to dumb down the connection of the soul out of protection. They had already experienced what it was like to access more than 10 percent of the soul while living within the limitations of fear.

Souls that expanded more than the 10 percent, found it hard to hide the access they had. These souls would isolate themselves, keeping themselves to themselves. Hiding the 100 percent access of the soul from the rest of the world.

When the soul decided to exit Earth, they left the creations behind, knowing one day they would be found. The soul knew exactly what it was doing by keeping it to itself. It knew what it created—a gift offered to Earth as a clue to help souls remember who they are.

Souls that found these creations regarded them as treasures even if they did not understand what they had found. These creations were locked away and passed down with each generation, resurfacing in the public domain after many centuries.

Souls often misinterpreted what they found and translated it with words that had been taught to them. These translations did not reflect the truth, and the meaning got lost in translation. The true meaning surfaced in the new paradigm. Souls understood the translation of the soul and discarded the translation of the mind.

Going back to come forward, these creations were no longer valued in money but valued in wisdom. The transition of the new paradigm opened up the pathway for the soul to connect 100 percent with the soul without the physical getting in the way, understanding that the life they once saw through the physical was not the truth after all.

Souls in the old paradigm had been so used to holding on, the challenge they faced during the shift was to let go of everything that they had been taught. This meant equally letting go of all the physical experiences that they had throughout each century, a process that took patience, as it was not a case of just dropping the past like letting go of a ball.

Souls had the physical mixed up with many souls reflected around them, like mixed balls of wool. Souls had to connect with their soul to unravel themselves, so that what they connected with only came from their own ball of energy. As souls accessed 100 percent of their soul, they found gifts within that transformed life on Earth. Earth connected with the many structures within the universe. Earth was no longer being used as a hotel. Souls were connected by the expansion of the soul. A soul wishing to visit Earth would do so if the frequency of the soul matched the frequency signature of structure Earth.

CHAPTER FOUR

OTHER STRUCTURES IN THE UNIVERSE

When I first gained access to 100 percent of my soul and viewed space around me, I became aware of how everything moved like every cell in the body. Each space of light that passed me was not a stationary star after all. The bigger picture of the universe surrounded me like a warm blanket. I recognized the frequencies of the universe that welcomed me home.

The pictures the old paradigm had of the universe were nothing like what I could see. The pictures the souls believed about the universe were like looking at a photograph of the physical body and saying the physical body never moved again after the picture was taken. This view of the universe was paused in time by what the soul believed in that moment.

Seeing the universe around me not only opened up my physical eyes, it opened up my soul. What had been hidden by the physical now became my way of life, a life I had kept to myself until now.

This booklet is an introduction and an invitation to you to connect with your soul so you can experience 100 percent of the universe for yourself. I did not have to physically travel anywhere on Earth; I did not have to search outside of my self to connect with my soul. I just chose to get off the rollercoaster ride, walked, and found a space to sit alone. I stayed in my soul in the space of my physical home.

I spent many years inside staying away from the distorted frequencies that passed my home like the wind during a storm. I knew I was not missing out on anything; I was content with what I accessed in my soul.

I worked from home doing soul readings throughout the world without ever having to leave my sofa. I travelled as much around Earth as I did the universe without physically moving. I used the frequency of my soul as my passport. I trusted the frequency of my soul to guide me no matter what faced me. I understood the souls around me were a mirror reflection.

I understood that I did not have to fear anything. I knew I was safe, even when the fear from other souls cast shadows on my wall. I knew nothing could touch me or harm me. I remembered that death did not exist.

I understood how the universe is a spiral of energy created by the souls' experiences. I knew nothing was personal; I didn't take the physical life seriously. I focused on what I knew and followed the pulse of my heart, which guided me on the soul path created by each choice I made. I chose to not follow the physical paths that had been carved out in fear; I knew they would not hold me.

I could see my soul path that other souls could not see. I had space from the physical frequency as I lived in my soul, a signature frequency that gave me 100 percent access to everything in the universe, which is why I was able to have access to your soul's reflection during a soul reading.

Souls that found me through word of mouth loved visiting the expanded space of my soul. This gave souls a safe place to connect with their own unique soul without the physical getting in the way. At first, souls that would book with me to have a soul reading thought they were visiting me with their physical body. Although the physical image of their body stared at me, I looked straight through the physical at their unique soul. I always knew whether they communicated with me from the space of soul or the physical frequency they had memorized so well.

Twin souls are like the soul dividing as it connects with the physical frequency of the body—two frequencies battling it out to be heard. The physical in the old paradigm received all the attention causing the soul to became a distant echo in space.

When I heard a frequency loud and clear, I would tune into this frequency avoiding the physical frequency they brought with them. At last the soul had some peace in which to open up and speak its truth. Reflected at me as I looked at their soul. I shared with them what their soul looked like, giving them confirmation of what they felt deep down inside, but feared it was their imagination.

Meeting Acho allowed me to share the 100 percent access of my soul. Souls felt free to explore their own soul and accessed what they were ready to receive. I felt the happiest I had ever been. Working without having to deal with the physical gave me the freedom to unlock other souls with the key of my soul—connecting soul to soul. I drew the image of the key of my soul frequency signature on a piece of paper, and my husband, Kevin, kindly made it by hand. I wear it proudly around my neck.

I knew soul readings where not for entertainment purposes or to pass a couple of hours away for the sake of curiosity.. Before a soul booked a soul reading, I had to make sure the soul was ready for the benefit of the soul and not the physical mind. I kindly asked souls to research the soul readings on my website, not because I was promoting my physical self, but because it was the only way I had of seeing how interested they were about the soul. I felt if they were interested enough to research it, then it was the soul driving them to do so and not their physical mind. I knew the physical mind was inpatient and wanted everything instantly, now, with minimal effort.

Some souls did not need to research my website, because they trusted the guidance they felt in their heart. This also confirmed to me that the decision to book a reading came from the connection of the heart and not the mind.

Soul readings became popular as a different doorway in which to access and connect with soul without the need of the physical as a prop. Souls that connected with me listened not to the sound of my voice but to the frequency tones from my soul. Connection only takes a nanosecond; often I did not even need to meet the physical to connect with the soul.

An open soul offers 100 percent access to my soul. I had even done a soul reading before the physical time slot on the day. When the physical arrives, I give them information that our souls had already shared. The physical is on catch up.

Soul readings are life changing, which is why I had to make sure that the bookings I made were from souls who were ready for change. The changes the souls went on to experience happened at their own pace. I knew the souls that connected in my space left without the physical weighing them down. They felt the frequency-transfer effects, which proved that the energy transfer from the physical frequency to the soul frequency was complete. They just had to get used to the access of 100 percent. Even if they did not explore the pool of the soul and only stood in it, they were still in 100 percent access of the soul pool regardless.

Going back to the physical way of life was not an option. If they tried to go back to the physical they had relinquished to connect with their soul, the pool would expand to remind them of where they were. No longer treading water of Earth, they were free to swim and explore the ocean of the soul. Whether standing or sitting or sleeping, they were still in the soul pool.

In the new paradigm, souls were open to understanding more about the universe and to remember Earth's connection and space. This opened up the map of the universe, and souls were able to view where their soul was in the bilocation of the map. The bilocation is the nearest frequency structure that matched their frequency.

The infinite map of the universe is created by soul. Each unique soul is expanding constantly with every thought that creates experience, which is what makes the universe space so infinite.

Letting go in your space does not mean you are forgetting who you are. Letting go means you wish to explore more than what you have already. Letting go means more not less.

Free falling in space is free. You do not have to pay anything. You do not owe anything. You have no debts.

You are the only soul in your space, which you share with yourself. No other soul forces you to experience anything that you do not wish to experience. You have the full right to your soul; your signature frequency is your copyright. If you wish to see nothing or do nothing more, then in nothing you are still in 100 percent access of your soul. It is no different from your children playing in a swimming pool and just standing still not bothering to swim. You know they still have access to 100 percent of the swimming pool if they so wish.

Each soul has a unique signature frequency that cannot be copied. You hold the key to your soul, which gives you total access. Just because you have not explored all of it does not mean it does not exist. What you experience will always be different from another soul. No matter which way you look at it, there are no carbon copies in the universe.

As you explore the universe, you will become aware that the map of the universe has been with you with every step you have taken while on Earth. It is in every blade of grass, in every tree, on your skin, within the design of your eyes, the flowers that you pick, and the animals that you feed. Every soul has the map of the universe,

You cannot get lost, for you are always in the comfort bubble of your soul space. The access of your soul that you share with the other souls you are sharing infinite space with depends on how much you wish to reflect. What you see is what you get; what you believe is what you get. There is only room for one soul in your unique frequency space, and that is you.

Master you, and then you have mastered the universe. What happens in the universe stays in the universe. Souls felt free because they understood the meaning of being alive. They knew they were not the physical body to which they chose to connect. Souls understood how life worked within the one language of the universe—the four elements of frequency—that played in the atmosphere of space for all to hear.

What I saw in a soul they too could now see. A soul looks like everything that you are, even the image of your physical body, because without energy the physical body would not exist. You bring everything about you with you via your soul. Connecting with the physical body is just another experience for your soul. Souls remember that they are the master of their own unique reality within the space of the soul.

Having faced what they called death during a soul reading, they instantly knew that death did not exist and was nothing to fear. Exiting Earth is a continuation because of the magic of space around each frequency.

They experienced more of themselves during a soul reading than they had previously physically accessed. They removed the limitation by accepting they had a choice: to either believe what they had been taught or to trust what they felt inside.

The soul has a strong magnetic pull; even the strongest of the fittest could not resist the attraction of the soul.

Souls had lost interest in the physical body, as it had run out of fresh, new experiences. Each soul was bored with repeats. For a fresh new start in the new paradigm, souls chose to take the soul path and let go of the physical path. Souls felt free and more alive than ever before; they did not feel the need to hold onto anything, not even the experiences they had chosen to have. They knew the soul deleted nothing.

They celebrated when a soul chose to exit Earth knowing they were continuing experiences in a different bilocation of their choice. Each soul knew that, no matter where they were in the universe, they never lost contact with anything.

Life on Earth became a fun place to enjoy with peace and love flowing from the heart in creative shared expression. Earth now had its own frequency signature that matched the souls visiting Earth for an experience.

Review Requested:

If you loved this book, would you please provide
a review at Amazon.com and Amazon.co.uk?

Lightning Source UK Ltd.
Milton Keynes UK
UKHW041139291121
394778UK00001B/149